COREY SEAGER

BASEBALL SUPERSTAR

BY DEREK MOON

Copyright © 2025 by Press Room Editions. All rights reserved. No part of this book may be used or reproduced in any manner whatsoever, including internet usage, without written permission from the copyright owner, except in the case of brief quotations embodied in critical articles and reviews.

Book design by Jake Nordby
Cover design by Jake Nordby

Photographs ©: Joe Robbins/Icon Sportswire/AP Images, cover, 1; Stacy Revere/Getty Images Sport/Getty Images, 4; Bailey Orr/Texas Rangers/Getty Images Sport/Getty Images, 6; Brian Westerholt/Sports On Film/AP Images, 8; Brace Hemmelgarn/Minnesota Twins/Getty Images Sport/Getty Images, 11; Denis Poroy/Getty Images Sport/Getty Images, 13; Harry How/Getty Images Sport/Getty Images, 14–15; Ezra Shaw/Getty Images Sport/Getty Images, 17; Sean M. Haffey/Getty Images Sport/Getty Images, 19; Tony Gutierrez/AP Images, 20–21, 30; Ron Jenkins/Getty Images Sport/Getty Images, 23; Sam Hodde/Getty Images Sport/Getty Images, 24; Rob Carr/Getty Images Sport/Getty Images, 26–27; Red Line Editorial, 29

Press Box Books, an imprint of Press Room Editions, Inc.

ISBN
978-1-63494-932-3 (library bound)
978-1-63494-937-8 (paperback)
978-1-63494-946-0 (epub)
978-1-63494-942-2 (hosted ebook)

Library of Congress Control Number: 2024939618

Distributed by North Star Editions, Inc.
2297 Waters Drive
Mendota Heights, MN 55120
www.northstareditions.com

Printed in the United States of America
082024

About the Author
Derek Moon is an author and avid Stratego player who lives in Watertown, Massachusetts, with his wife and daughter.

TABLE OF CONTENTS

CHAPTER 1
World Series Star 5

CHAPTER 2
Carolina Kid 9

CHAPTER 3
Dodger Dynamo 15

CHAPTER 4
Taking on Texas 21

SPECIAL FEATURE
Fast Start 26

Timeline • 28
At a Glance • 30
Glossary • 31
To Learn More • 32
Index • 32

1 WORLD SERIES STAR

Corey Seager dug his feet into the batter's box. The opposing pitcher threw a fastball toward the top of the strike zone. That was a big mistake. In one powerful motion, Seager drove the ball into the sky. It landed 418 feet away in the right field stands.

Seager doesn't show a lot of emotion when he plays. But this moment was special. Running to first base, he turned to his Texas Rangers teammates in the dugout and let out a roar. The

Corey Seager's home run in Game 1 of the 2023 World Series was his 17th career postseason home run.

Seager couldn't contain his emotions after blasting the game-tying home run against the Diamondbacks.

Arizona Diamondbacks had been two outs away from winning Game 1 of the 2023 World Series. But Seager's two-run homer tied the game in the bottom of the ninth inning. Texas went on to win 6-5 in the 11th.

Seager was already one of the league's best shortstops. However, he raised his game in the World Series. He smashed two more homers against the Diamondbacks. He drove in six runs. In Game 5, he broke up a no-hitter in the seventh inning. Texas went on to win that game 5-0. For the first time in team history, the Rangers were champions. And for the second time in four seasons, Seager won the World Series Most Valuable Player (MVP) Award.

ELITE COMPANY

The World Series MVP Award was created in 1955. Corey Seager became only the fourth player to win it twice. Pitchers Sandy Koufax and Bob Gibson both did it in the 1960s. Outfielder Reggie Jackson did it in the 1970s. Seager and Jackson both won the award with two different teams.

2 CAROLINA KID

Corey Seager was born on April 27, 1994. His hometown of Kannapolis, North Carolina, is in the heart of NASCAR country. But baseball ruled the Seager house. All three boys were great players. The Seattle Mariners drafted Kyle Seager. Justin Seager went on to play in the minor leagues. Corey Seager looked like he could be the best of the three, though.

The family lived on a farm. As a kid, Corey had to help with chores. But he never complained. Corey took the

On top of baseball, Corey Seager also played three years of varsity basketball in high school.

same approach in the classroom and on the baseball field.

Corey attended Northwest Cabarrus High School. Teammates thought of Corey as quiet and respectful. His play spoke for itself. Corey had speed and strength. At shortstop, he rarely made mistakes. But it was his smooth left-handed swing that set him apart. In one game, he blasted a home run over some trees beyond the outfield wall.

Corey was a senior in 2012. By then, opposing pitchers had learned not to throw him many strikes. Yet he still hit .519 with 10 home runs. After the season, he was named North Carolina's player of the year. Corey decided to play baseball at the University of

In 2014, Corey Seager played in an all-star game for baseball's best prospects.

South Carolina. That plan changed in June 2012. The Los Angeles Dodgers picked him 18th in the Major League Baseball (MLB) Draft. Then they offered him $2.35 million.

So, Seager packed his bags and headed for the minor leagues.

Seager began his minor league career in Ogden, Utah. Over the next three years, he quickly moved up to better leagues. Scouts loved his natural talent and mature approach. Then, in late 2015, the Dodgers called him up.

On September 3, Seager made his major league

HIGH SCHOOL SWEETHEARTS

Corey Seager and Madisyn Van Ham attended senior prom together in 2012. Then Seager left for the minor leagues after high school. The two kept in touch. Eventually, they began dating again. In 2019, Seager proposed to Van Ham at a New England Patriots game. He had always wanted to see the team's star quarterback, Tom Brady. The couple got married a year later.

Seager slides into home during his MLB debut.

debut against the San Diego Padres. Despite being only 21, Seager looked more than ready for the big leagues. He hit a double in his second at-bat. Later in the game, he hit a single. He also scored a pair of runs while driving in two more. Seager's promising career was only beginning.

3 DODGER DYNAMO

Shortstop is a difficult position to play. A shortstop has to be quick and agile in the field. At 6-foot-4 (193 cm) and 215 pounds (98 kg), Corey Seager was big for the position. Some scouts wondered if he should play third base. However, Seager's success in the minor leagues showed that he could handle shortstop. Plus, few shortstops could hit like he did.

Each year, experts rank baseball's top prospects. In 2016, the four major rankings all put Seager at the top of the

Seager played six games at third base in 2015. The Dodgers made him their full-time shortstop in 2016.

15

list. He quickly lived up to the hype. In one game, he hit three homers. No Dodgers rookie had done that since 1959. Seager made the All-Star Game in 2016. He ended the year with a .308 batting average and 26 home runs. Only two players received more votes for the National League (NL) MVP Award. But every voter agreed that Seager was the NL Rookie of the Year.

Seager made his second All-Star Game in 2017. Then he helped the Dodgers reach the World Series. However, Los Angeles fell to the Houston Astros in seven games. The Dodgers made it back to the World Series in 2018. But this time, Seager couldn't play. Injuries forced him to miss most of the season. All he could

Seager screams after hitting a home run during the 2017 World Series.

do was watch as the Boston Red Sox beat the Dodgers in five games.

In 2020, Seager was healthy again. And nothing could stop him in the playoffs. The Dodgers swept their first two series. Then Los Angeles played the Atlanta Braves in the NL Championship Series (NLCS). In seven games, Seager blasted five home runs. And he drove in 11 runs. Both were NLCS records. Seager was named NLCS MVP. Most importantly, the Dodgers advanced to their third World Series in four seasons.

BROTHERLY SLUGS

Third baseman Kyle Seager joined the Seattle Mariners in 2011. Nine years later, brothers Kyle and Corey Seager met for the first time in an MLB game. On August 17, 2020, Corey blasted a three-run homer in the bottom of the second inning. Kyle answered with a solo homer in the top of the third. The Dodgers went on to win 11–9.

Seager drove in 20 runs during the 2020 postseason, coming up just one shy of the record.

Seager's aggressive base running helped the Dodgers win Game 1. He drilled a home run in Game 2. Then he went 4-for-5 with another homer in Game 4. In total, he hit .400 while driving in five runs and scoring seven. The Dodgers beat the Tampa Bay Rays in six games. Seager's MVP performance lifted Los Angeles to its first title in 32 years.

4 TAKING ON TEXAS

The 2020 World Series had shown the best of Corey Seager. He followed that up with another strong season in 2021. However, injuries once again slowed him down. Seager played in just 95 games. It seemed like the only thing that could stop Seager was his body.

Seager became a free agent after that season. That meant he could join any team. In a surprise to many, he signed with the Texas Rangers. Leaving Los Angeles was a risky choice. Seager had become

Seager hit 33 home runs in each of his first two seasons with Texas.

a star with the Dodgers. They were one of baseball's most successful teams. They came into every season as World Series contenders. Meanwhile, Texas had just finished its fifth losing season in a row. And Rangers fans could only dream of celebrating a championship.

The team had big plans, though. The Rangers had recently built a new ballpark. They also signed some All-Star free agents. None was bigger than Seager. He agreed to a massive 10-year, $325 million deal.

The challenge of turning the team around motivated Seager. However, winning in Texas proved to be difficult. The Rangers had gone 60–102 the year before Seager arrived. In his first season with the team, they won only eight

Seager turned a career-high 91 double plays in 2022.

Seager lifts the World Series trophy during the Rangers' championship parade in 2023.

more games. Seager had one of his worst seasons at the plate. Then, two weeks into the 2023 season, disaster struck. Seager strained his hamstring and missed 31 games.

The tough start didn't hold him down. Once he came back, Seager began crushing the ball with ease. He went on to put up career-best numbers. Just as importantly, the team was on the rise. The Rangers had a strong mix of young and veteran players. They helped Texas win 90 games.

The team made the playoffs for the first time in seven years. That's when Seager took over. With his dominant World Series performance, he lifted the Rangers to their first championship. It had only taken two years for Seager to help turn the Rangers into winners. And at 29, he was still at the top of his game.

GIVING BACK

Senter Park is a small park near the Rangers' stadium. Many kids play baseball there. In 2024, Corey Seager donated new batting cages to the park. Giving back to the community has always been important to Seager. Even in high school, he volunteered with local organizations, including a children's hospital. As a big leaguer, he has supported causes in Los Angeles, Texas, and North Carolina.

FAST START

The 2023 American League Championship Series came down to a winner-take-all Game 7. Corey Seager got the Rangers on the board early. In the top of the first, he blasted a 440-foot home run. Texas stayed hot after that. The Rangers crushed the Houston Astros 11–4. That win sent Texas to the World Series.

TIMELINE

1. Charlotte, North Carolina (April 27, 1994)
Corey Seager is born.

2. Kannapolis, North Carolina (2012)
Corey is named North Carolina's high school player of the year.

3. Ogden, Utah (July 6, 2012)
Seager begins his professional baseball career with the Ogden Raptors in the Pioneer League, a minor league for rookies.

4. San Diego, California (September 3, 2015)
Seager makes his major league debut with the Los Angeles Dodgers. He goes 2-for-4 and drives in two runs.

5. Los Angeles, California (June 3, 2016)
Seager hits three home runs in a 4–2 win over the Atlanta Braves. He goes on to hit 26 homers that season and wins the NL Rookie of the Year Award.

6. Arlington, Texas (October 27, 2020)
Seager is named World Series MVP after leading the Dodgers to their first championship in 32 years.

7. Arlington, Texas (December 1, 2021)
Seager signs with the Texas Rangers.

8. Phoenix, Arizona (November 1, 2023)
The Rangers beat the Arizona Diamondbacks to claim their first World Series championship. Seager wins his second World Series MVP Award.

MAP

29

AT A GLANCE

Birth date: April 27, 1994

Birthplace: Charlotte, North Carolina

Position: Shortstop

Throws: Right

Bats: Left

Size: 6-foot-4 (193 cm), 215 pounds (98 kg)

Current team: Texas Rangers (2022–)

Previous team: Los Angeles Dodgers (2015–21)

Major awards: NL Rookie of the Year (2016), All-Star (2016–17, 2022–23), Silver Slugger (2016–17, 2023), World Series MVP (2020, 2023)

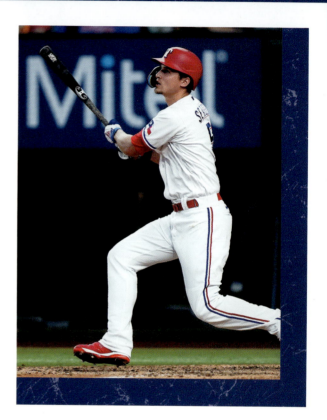

Accurate through the 2023 season.

GLOSSARY

agile
Able to move quickly and gracefully.

contenders
Teams that are good enough to win a title.

debut
First appearance.

drafted
Selected an athlete in an event that allows teams to choose new players coming into the league.

fastball
A pitch thrown at a pitcher's top speed.

free agent
A player who can sign with any team.

prospects
Players that people expect to do well at a higher level.

rookie
A first-year player.

scouts
People who look for talented young players.

veteran
A player who has spent several years in a league.

TO LEARN MORE

Books

Calcaterra, Craig. *Stars of Major League Baseball*. New York: Abbeville Press Publishers, 2023.

Donnelly, Patrick. *Texas Rangers*. Minneapolis: Abdo Publishing, 2023.

Olson, Ethan. *Great MLB World Series Championships*. San Diego: BrightPoint Press, 2024.

More Information

To learn more about Corey Seager, go to **pressboxbooks.com/AllAccess**.

These links are routinely monitored and updated to provide the most current information available.

INDEX

All-Star Game, 16
Arizona Diamondbacks, 6–7
Atlanta Braves, 18

Boston Red Sox, 18
Brady, Tom, 12

Gibson, Bob, 7

Houston Astros, 16, 26

Jackson, Reggie, 7

Koufax, Sandy, 7

MLB Draft, 12

New England Patriots, 12
Northwest Cabarrus High School, 10

San Diego Padres, 13
Seager, Justin, 9
Seager, Kyle, 9, 18
Seattle Mariners, 9, 18

Tampa Bay Rays, 19

Van Ham, Madisyn, 12